RECORD-BREAKING EARTH FACTS

And the SCIENCE behind them!

Izzi Howell

WAYLAND

First published in Great Britain in 2026 by Wayland
Copyright © Hodder & Stoughton Limited, 2026
Produced for Wayland by

All rights reserved.

Editor: Izzi Howell
Designer: Clare Nicholas

HB ISBN: 978 1 5263 2945 5
PB ISBN: 978 1 5263 2946 2

Wayland
An imprint of
Hachette Children's Group
Part of Hodder & Stoughton Limited
Carmelite House
50 Victoria Embankment
London EC4Y 0DZ

An Hachette UK Company
www.hachette.co.uk
www.hachettechildrens.co.uk

The authorised representative in the EEA is Hachette Ireland, 8 Castlecourt Centre, Dublin 15, D15 XTP3, Ireland (email: info@hbgi.ie)

FSC MIX Paper | Supporting responsible forestry FSC® C104740

Printed in Dubai

Picture acknowledgements:
Ground Truth Trekking 7b; NASA Earth Observatory image by Lauren Dauphin 6r; Shutterstock: Jr images, Mark Bridger, Photoongraphy, astudio, Breyenn, domnitsky, Marti Bug Catcher, Tomas Ragina, Dotted Yeti, Sendo Serra, Shutterstock AI Generator and Zoart Studio cover, ymphotos 3t and 13t, Marti Bug Catcher 3b and 14-15, Fotos593 4, M. Rinandar Tasya 5t, Moriz 5b, ianmitchinson 6-7, owatta 7t, Thomas Heyer 8-9, Zern Liew 9t, Karin Wassmer 9b, Oasishifi, chrisbrignell, Mega Vectors, Rosa Jay, Aastels, Passakorn Umpornmaha, Ana Vasileva, GoodStudio and Anton_Ivanov 10-11, Elizaveta Galitckaia 12, AntiMartina 13b, Marcus Placidus 15l, Igor Zakowski 15r, Mozgova 16-17, Janelle Lugge 17t, Davidenco 17b, Cavan-Images 18-19, Allied Computer Graphics 19t, AntonSokolov 19b, chonlasub woravichan 20 and 30b, ChameleonsEye 21l, Ekaterina Mikheeva 21r, Tatyana Andreyeva 22-23, Vectorium 23t, Alexey Kharitonov 23b, alejojimenezyt 24, Dmitry Shanchuk 25t, Douglas Olivares 25b, yanikap 26-27, matunka 26t, Myshkovskyi 26c, Sararoom Design 27b, Kichigin 28t, Tatiana Kovaleva 28c, Social Media HUB 28b, Stephen Moehle 29t, Alexandree 29b, Dotted Yeti 30t, Anton_Ivanov 31; Wikimedia: Pedroalexandrade 28c.
All design elements from Shutterstock.

The website addresses (URLs) included in this book were valid at the time of going to press. However, it is possible that contents or addresses may have changed since the publication of this book. No responsibility for any such changes can be accepted by either the author or the publisher.

All facts and statistics were correct at the time of press.

MEASUREMENTS

Keep track of all the measurements in the book with this handy guide!

cm = centimetre
m = metre
km = kilometre
g = gram
kg = kilogram

Contents

Explosive eruption 4
Wave power 6
Dusty and dry 8
So many species 10
Speedy breeze 12
Mighty mountain 14
Cool as ice 16
Burn, baby, burn 18
Champion coral 20
Dark depths 22
Waterfall wonder 24
Plant power 26
More incredible earth records 28
Glossary 30
Further information 31
Index 32

Explosive ERUPTION

MOST POWERFUL ERUPTION

Time travellers beware! Stay well clear of **MOUNT TAMBORA** in Indonesia. Back in 1815, this volcano was the site of the most powerful volcanic eruption in recorded history.

Small shakes and thundering rumbles were the first clues of the devastating eruption that was to follow.

Then, Mount Tambora blasted open, releasing around 150 cubic km of ash, rock and gas. Deadly pyroclastic flows made up of hot gas, ash and rock sped down the slopes, covering areas up to 20 km away.

🌊 ERUPTION ISSUES

The effects of the eruption spread far beyond the immediate area. Huge amounts of rock were launched into the sea, which triggered towering tsunamis that flooded the coastlines of nearby islands. Ash rained down in many places, destroying crops and poisoning drinking water, which left people hungry and thirsty.

Mount Tambora's massive caldera (crater) left by its 1815 eruption can be seen today. The volcano is still active and is carefully monitored by scientists in case of any future eruptions.

❄ DARK AND COLD

The eruption of Mount Tambora released a massive amount of sulfur gas into the atmosphere. This gas blocked light and heat from the Sun, lowering temperatures worldwide by about 3°C. Things got so chilly that 1816, the year following the eruption, was known as 'the year without a summer'!

Mount Tambora exploded with so much force that it lost over 1,400 m of its height during the eruption, creating a massive 6-km-wide crater.

🏆 DID YOU KNOW?

Cover your ears! The eruption of Mount Tambora was so explosive that it could be heard almost 2,000 km away in Australia!

What was that?

WAVE POWER

TALLEST WAVE

Can you imagine a wave as high as a 150-storey skyscraper?! The normally quiet Lituya Bay in Alaska, USA, experienced just that when a mega-tsunami came crashing through in 1958. It hit the shore at **524 M** above sea level, devastating almost everything in its path.

The mega-tsunami that hit Lituya Bay was set off by an enormous landslide. A massive chunk of the high cliffs that surround the bay fell into the water following a powerful earthquake.

An aerial view of Lituya Bay

When the rock fell into the bay, it made the water level rise dramatically. This is due to displacement (find out more on page 7).

The shape of the bay also affected the height of the wave. Normally, tsunamis spread out in a fan shape, but the narrow width and tall sides of the bay made this impossible. Instead, the water was forced even higher upwards, resulting in a terribly tall tsunami.

DISPLACEMENT DANGERS

Have you ever noticed how the water level rises when you get into a bath full of water? Ever wondered why? That's right - displacement! When an object is placed into a liquid, the liquid is pushed out of the way to create space for the object. The amount of liquid displaced is equal to the volume of the object, so a lot of rock equals a *lot* of displaced water!

DID YOU KNOW?

The amount of rock that fell during the landslide would have been enough to fill 10,000 Olympic-sized swimming pools!

MORE MEGA-TSUNAMIS?

The shape of the coastline near Lituya Bay, with lots of narrow inlets with steep sides created by glaciers, make it a mega-tsunami hotspot. In 2015, the nearby Taan fjord experienced another, slightly smaller mega-tsunami, which reached heights of over 190 m tall (the equivalent of a 60 storey building!).

As in Lituya Bay, the Taan fjord mega-tsunami stripped away plants and forests all along the shore, leaving behind bare beaches.

DUSTY AND DRY

DRIEST NON-POLAR DESERT

If you ever visit the **ATACAMA DESERT**, you can leave your raincoat at home! Receiving less than 5 mm of rain per year, it's the driest place on Earth, apart from the polar deserts that cover the inland part of Antarctica.

The Atacama Desert is particularly dry because it lies between two mountain chains, which creates a double rain shadow effect. This is when rain mostly falls on one side of a mountain, leaving the other side extremely dry. Now imagine that times two!

Winds that blow across the Atacama Desert are cooled by the Pacific Ocean, which means that they aren't the right temperature to pick up moisture from the sea. As a result, they don't carry any water to drop as rain.

No rain = no clouds = no problem spotting stars! As a result, the Atacama Desert is the perfect spot for astronomy and is home to several observatories.

DID YOU KNOW?

There are weather stations in the Atacama Desert that have never recorded rain!

I'm still waiting...

Weather station rain collector

LIFE IN THE DESERT

Some parts of the Atacama are too dry to support any life, but plants and animals, such as grasshoppers, cacti and scorpions, manage to survive around the edges of the driest areas. More species are found around the outskirts of the desert, where they can find moisture from ocean fog and melted snow.

The viscacha (a relative of the chinchilla) feeds on the grass, moss and lichens found in less dry parts of the Atacama Desert.

SCIENCE AND SPACE

Scientists use the Atacama Desert to test equipment and vehicles designed for use on Mars, as the dry and dusty conditions in both places are very similar! They have also found microbes able to survive in the driest parts of the desert, which might help them with their search for life in 'inhospitable' parts of space.

SO MANY SPECIES

MOST BIODIVERSITY

When it comes to biodiversity (the variety of life on Earth), the AMAZON RAINFOREST is head and shoulders above any other habitat! This South American rainforest covers just 1 per cent of our planet's surface but contains at least 10 per cent of all species that live on Earth.

SO MANY SPECIES

The Amazon Rainforest is home to millions of different species of plants, insects, birds, mammals, reptiles and probably many more that we don't know about yet! These animals live on and around over 2,500 different species of tree.

Collared anteater

Leaf cutter ants

The rainforest is so biodiverse because it has different layers, such as the forest floor, the canopy of branches and the tops of trees. Each layer creates multiple mini habitats with different conditions and contains many species that are adapted to the conditions there.

Green anaconda

SPEEDY BREEZE

FASTEST WIND

Wind can be annoying enough at its regular speed of 6 to 11 km per hour, let alone at its fastest ever recorded speed of **408 KM PER HOUR**. That's faster than a speeding arrow!

This gigantic gust was measured on an island off the coast of Australia during a tropical cyclone in 1996. It was picked up by a machine called an anemometer, which is used to calculate wind speed and direction.

Tropical cyclones are fast, swirling storms that start over warm, tropical oceans. As well as extremely strong winds, they also bring torrential rain.

Tropical cyclones get stronger the longer they spend over the ocean, as they get their energy from heat and evaporating water from the sea. They hit islands and coastlines with great force and then become weaker as they move inland.

 ALL IN THE NAME

Did you know that tropical cyclones, hurricanes and typhoons are all the same type of storm? Their name just depends on their location. Hurricanes are found in the Atlantic Ocean or northeast Pacific Ocean, typhoons happen in the northwest Pacific Ocean and tropical cyclones occur in the Indian Ocean and southern Pacific Ocean.

Tropical cyclones can be incredibly destructive. This is the aftermath of a typhoon that hit the Philippines.

EVEN FASTER?

Scientists believe that wind may reach even greater speeds inside tornadoes. However, it's understandably very hard for them to measure wind speed without having their equipment broken apart by the tornado's violent gusts!

 DID YOU KNOW?

Skyscrapers are designed to gently sway with the breeze so that they aren't blown over by strong winds.

Mighty MOUNTAIN

TALLEST MOUNTAIN

Climbers who reach the peak of **MOUNT EVEREST** must know what it's like to be on top of the world! The peak of this mammoth mountain sits at 8,849 m above sea level, making it the tallest mountain on Earth.

Mount Everest is part of the Himalayan mountain chain. Many other nearby mountains are close in height to Everest, but none are tall enough to snatch Everest's crown.

The Himalayan mountains formed about 40 to 50 million years ago when the tectonic plate containing India collided with the Eurasian tectonic plate. The force of the impact pushed up the land into tall mountain peaks.

Due to Everest's height and extreme conditions, very few animals or plants live near its peak. However, bears, snow leopards and birds are found on its lower slopes.

☠ DEADLY ADVENTURE

Mount Everest is popular with adventurous climbers who want to claim they have reached the top of Earth's highest mountain. However, conditions on the mountain are extremely dangerous and it has claimed the lives of over 300 climbers.

WHO'S THE WINNER?

Everest takes first prize when measured from sea level, but if we were to count beneath sea level, Mauna Kea in Hawaii would be number one. Mauna Kea in Hawaii is only 4,205 m above sea level, but if you measure its height from its base on the sea floor, it's a massive 10,200 m tall, beating Everest outright!

Avalanches and blizzards are common on Mount Everest. Climbers also face dangers such as hypothermia, frostbite, snow blindness and lack of oxygen.

DID YOU KNOW?

A species of jumping spider has been discovered living on Mount Everest at heights of up to 6,700 m high. This makes it the highest living non-microscopic animal on Earth!

Can't beat the view from up here!

Cool as ICE

MOST FRESH WATER

Feeling thirsty? Head south! The **ANTARCTIC ICE SHEET** contains the largest reserve of fresh water on Earth. The only problem is that you'll need to melt the ice to get a drink of water!

The Antarctic ice sheet contains over 60 per cent of all fresh water available on Earth. Almost all the rest is locked away in other glaciers or as groundwater, with only a very small amount available as fresh liquid water in rivers and lakes.

The ice sheet is formed of layers of frost and snow that build up on the surface over time. The weight of the upper layers presses down on the lower layers, compacting them into thick ice.

The Antarctic ice sheet isn't just big … it's also very thick. It has an average thickness of 2 km, which is about six and a half times the height of the Eiffel Tower!

LAND AND SEA

The massive ice sheet covers nearly the entire continent of Antarctica and also extends onto the sea in some parts of the coast, creating a floating ice shelf.

DID YOU KNOW?

The sea around Antarctica also freezes in winter. The addition of sea ice around Antarctica almost doubles the size of the ice sheet!

Icebergs are formed when chunks of the ice shelf fall away. This process is happening more frequently because of global warming.

Where did all this ice come from?

MELTING AWAY

Global warming is leading to extreme ice loss on the Antarctic ice sheet. Scientists estimate that around 135 billion tonnes of Antarctic ice are melting into the oceans every year. This is making sea levels rise around the world, leading to flooding along the coasts.

Burn, Baby, Burn

HOTTEST AIR TEMPERATURE

In the summer, **DEATH VALLEY** in California, USA, becomes the hottest place on Earth. It's here that the highest ever air temperature was recorded - a sweltering 56.7 °C! So, why is Death Valley so ridiculously hot?

Death Valley is located in the Mojave Desert. Here, skies are always clear as there is very little rain. As a result, there are no clouds to block the Sun's rays, so their full strength heats the air and ground.

Hot desert winds also blow up the valley, increasing temperatures even further.

The steep sides of the valley trap warm air and redirect it back towards the burning desert floor where it is heated all over again. Over time, this air gets hotter and hotter!

DID YOU KNOW?

Death Valley was given its name by settlers who got lost in the area in the 1850s and believed they would die there from thirst and hunger. Luckily, almost all of them managed to make it out alive!

"At least you don't have to pull this wagon!"

AIR OR GROUND?

When monitoring temperature, scientists usually take readings from the air and from the ground. However, temperatures taken on the ground can easily be 30 to 50 °C hotter than air temperatures as the ground can absorb more heat than the air.

SALTY SURPRISE

Despite the area's dry reputation, a saltwater lake covered Death Valley in prehistoric times. The lake evaporated away over time, leaving behind large amounts of salt. This salt can still be seen today in large, white salt flats that cover parts of Death Valley.

The crust of salt covering parts of Death Valley ranges from 3 cm to 1.5 m deep!

Champion CORAL

LARGEST LIVING STRUCTURE

Spanning over 2,000 km off the north-eastern coast of Australia, the **GREAT BARRIER REEF** is the largest living structure on Earth. It's hard to believe, but this interconnecting network of coral reefs is so large that it can be seen from space!

Coral may look like a plant but it's actually a group of tiny animals called coral polyps that live and grow together in colonies.

The Great Barrier Reef is made up of nearly 3,000 separate coral reefs. Some of them are located around islands or along the coast, while others are offshore.

BRILLIANT BIODIVERSITY

The Great Barrier Reef is a biodiverse area, home to a huge number of different species of coral, fish, shellfish, sea turtles and much more! However, one of its residents, the crown-of-thorn starfish, is a major threat to the reefs, as it feeds on and destroys the coral polyps.

Each coral polyp grows a hard exoskeleton around its soft insides. New polyps grow on top of the exoskeletons left by previous generations, which slowly creates hard pieces of coral.

⚠ REEF AT RISK

Sadly, starfish aren't the only threat facing the Great Barrier Reef. Changes in ocean temperature linked to climate change, pollution and overfishing are all putting this unique and record-breaking reef in danger.

Tourist numbers at the Great Barrier Reef must be carefully monitored as visitors can damage the coral and other animals that live on the reef.

DID YOU KNOW?

The bright colours of coral actually come from tiny algae that live inside coral polyps!

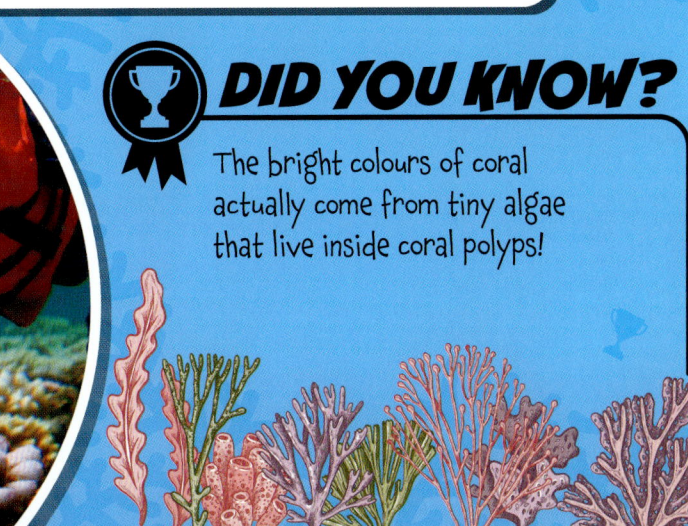

DARK DEPTHS

DEEPEST LAKE

If you ever feel anxious about swimming in deep water, stay close to the edges of **LAKE BAIKAL**! This Russian lake is up to 1,620 m deep in places, which is equivalent to the height of 17 Big Ben towers! And who knows what's lurking at the bottom ...

Don't worry – there's nothing sinister in Lake Baikal! The lake is actually a very biodiverse area, with a huge number of different species of fish, birds and invertebrates, many of which aren't found anywhere else on Earth.

Lake Baikal is a multiple medal winner, also holding the records for largest freshwater lake by volume *and* the oldest lake on Earth, at around 20 to 25 million years old.

More than 330 rivers and streams flow into Lake Baikal, contributing to its massive volume of water.

THANKS TO TECTONICS!

Lake Baikal formed when tectonic plates moved away from each other, leaving a sunken area. The basin filled with water and hey presto, Lake Baikal was born! There is still a lot of tectonic activity in the area with hot springs heated by cracks in Earth's crust and the occasional earthquake.

DID YOU KNOW?

Lake Baikal is slightly larger than the country Belgium!

No way!

ALL YEAR ROUND

The surface of Lake Baikal freezes for several months during the winter and spring. In the summer and autumn, storms are common and massive waves appear on the lake.

Baikal seals give birth to their pups in winter so that their young can stay on the ice until they are ready to swim in the water.

Waterfall WONDER

TALLEST WATERFALL

It's a long way down from the top of **Angel Falls**, Venezuela - 979 m to be exact! For comparison, that's about two and a half times the height of the Empire State Building in New York City, USA.

At Angel Falls, water from the Churún River drops over the towering edge of Auyán-Tepuí, a flat-topped plateau.

Angel Falls has such a powerful stream that it barely touches the cliff face behind it.

The high volume of water in Angel Falls is thanks to heavy rainfall on top of the plateau. This mainly falls in the rainy season between June and September.

FALLS FORMATION

Waterfalls like Angel Falls form when water flows over an area of both hard and soft rock. The movement of the water erodes the area of soft rock, creating a drop in level between the hard and soft rock. The result? A wonderful waterfall!

DID YOU KNOW?

Although Angel Falls may look heavenly, it's actually named after James Angel, a US explorer who was the first person to fly over the falls in 1933!

Woah, what's that down there?

TOURIST TROUBLES

With its stunning scenery, it's no surprise that Angel Falls is a popular tourist attraction. However, it is very hard to reach, as it is located deep within an isolated rainforest with no road access. Visitors usually fly in by plane and then travel along the river to reach the falls.

Travelling to Angel Falls by boat gives visitors an excellent view. Just make sure you travel along the river at the bottom and not off the top!

Plant POWER

LARGEST MASS

Which living thing takes up the most space on Earth? Giant whales? Tons of tiny insects? Believe it or not, it's actually **PLANTS** that rule our planet when it comes to their mass!

Creatures in Common

All living things, whether they are plants, animals, bacteria or fungi, share certain characteristics, including growing, moving and needing food. If you go way back, all living things share a common ancestor (probably a very simple single-celled organism) and, most importantly for this topic, all living things contain carbon.

Each group of living things is built differently. For example, bacteria are microorganisms, often made up of just one cell, while animals are made up of many different types of cell.

Scientists use the quantity of carbon inside a living thing as a measure of its mass. In total, all the living things alive on Earth today contain around 550 gigatons of carbon (550,000 billion kilograms).

PEOPLE PROBLEMS

Humans make up just 0.06 gigatons of the carbon found in living things but we have a massive impact on the natural world. Scientists believe that before humans started farming, there were double the number of plants on Earth.

If you combined the carbon found in all plants, it would add up to a staggering 450 gigatons! That's 81 per cent of all carbon found in living things, making plants easily the most dominant living thing by mass on our planet.

Plants are followed by bacteria (70 gigatons) and fungi (12 gigatons). These often-overlooked living things actually perform many important tasks, such as helping to break down the remains of other living things.

DID YOU KNOW?

Both molluscs (snails, octopuses and shellfish) and livestock are much greater in mass than humans!

So we're outnumbered by snails?

humans (0.06 gigatons)

livestock (0.1 gigatons)

molluscs (0.2 gigatons)

MORE INCREDIBLE

RAINIEST PLACE

If you ever visit the village of **MĀWSYNRĀM** in northeastern India, you better bring an umbrella! This area gets around 12 m of rain a year, most of which falls during the monsoon season, but has been known to receive over 1 m of rain in just one day!

DEEPEST CAVE

The **VERYOVKINA CAVE** in Georgia is at least 2,212 m deep – that's two and a half times as high as the Burj Khalifa, the tallest building in the world! It took explorers more than four days to reach the bottom. However, it's possible that the cave may be even deeper.

LONGEST LIGHTNING BOLT

At an unbelievable **767 KM** long, the longest known lightning bolt stretched across three US states! However, it didn't touch the ground at any point, jumping instead from cloud to cloud. This type of horizontal lightning, known as a megaflash, happens during very intense storms.

EARTH RECORDS

TALLEST LIVING TREE

The coast redwood **HYPERION** is a massive 116 m tall, more than the Statue of Liberty! Coast redwoods are known for being some of the tallest trees on Earth. Hyperion has also had plenty of time to grow, as it is thought to be between 600 and 800 years old.

OLDEST ROCK

Rock from the **ACASTA GNEISS** in Canada is the oldest rock on Earth at 4 billion years old! For comparison, Earth itself is around 4.5 billion years old. Earth's rocks are constantly being 'recycled' through the rock cycle, so it's unusual for a piece of rock to have lasted this long.

LONGEST RIVER

THE NILE, in Africa, has traditionally been considered to be the longest river in the world at 6,650 km, but some scientists claim that the Amazon, in South America, is actually longer! It all depends on what you consider to be the source of the Amazon. Scientists are continuing to study the issue, using the latest satellite analysis to help them with their research.

Glossary

atmosphere the mixture of gas and air above Earth

biodiversity the variety of different species of living things

canopy the overlapping branches and leaves at the top of trees in a forest

carbon an element found in all living things

climate change changes in the world's weather, in particular an increase in temperature, which scientists believe are mainly due to human activity

colony a group of the same type of animals that live together

crater a round hole in the ground

erode to wear away (rock)

evaporate when a liquid evaporates, it turns into a gas

exoskeleton a hard, outer layer that protects the outside of some invertebrates (animals without backbones)

global warming an increase in temperatures on Earth

groundwater water found beneath Earth's surface

monsoon a season of heavy rain

sea level the average height of the sea where it meets the land

source the starting point of a river

tectonic plate a section of Earth's crust

understorey the lower branches that are found beneath the canopy in a forest

Further Information

Books

Big Planet by Jon Richards and Josy Bloggs
(Franklin Watts, 2024)

The Wow and How of Planet Earth by Thora Hagen
(Wayland, 2024)

You Choose: Planet Earth by Izzi Howell
(Wayland, 2024)

Websites

Discover some more amazing facts about weather
www.natgeokids.com/uk/discover/geography/physical-geography/30-freaky-facts-about-weather/

Learn more about desert habitats
kids.britannica.com/kids/article/desert/346108

Explore some of the natural wonders of the world
easyscienceforkids.com/all-about-the-natural-wonders-of-the-world/

Index

Amazon Rainforest 10-11
Angel Falls 24-25
animals 9, 10, 11, 14, 15, 20, 21, 22, 23, 26, 27
Antarctica 8, 16-17
Atacama Desert 8-9

bacteria 26, 27
biodiversity 10, 11, 21, 22

carbon 26-27
caves 28
climate change 11, 21
coral 20-21
cyclones 12, 13

Death Valley 18-19
deserts 8, 9, 18

flooding 5, 17
freshwater 16, 22

global warming 17
Great Barrier Reef 20-21

Hyperion (tree) 29

ice 16, 17, 23

Lake Baikal 22-23
landslide 6, 7
lightning 28

Māwsynrām 28
Mount Everest 14-15
Mount Tambora 4-5

Nile River 29

plants 9, 10, 11, 14, 26, 27, 29

rain 8, 9, 12, 18, 25, 28
rivers 16, 22, 24, 25, 29
rock 4, 5, 6, 7, 25, 29

salt 19
storms 12, 13, 23, 28

tectonic plates 14, 23
temperature 5, 8, 18, 19, 21
tsunamis 5, 6-7

Veryovkina Cave 28
volcanoes 4-5

waves 6-7, 23
wind 8, 12-13, 18

TITLES IN THE SERIES

- Sprint at speed
- Champion snoozer
- Mighty muncher
- Harmful hunter
- Top twister
- Powerful poison
- Cool climber
- Underwater roar
- Need for speed
- Super furry animal
- Marathon migrator
- Skilled sniffer
- More incredible animal records

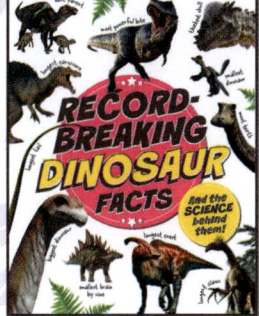

- Diverse dinos
- Bone-crushing bite
- Baby brain
- Claw-some lengths
- Small-o-saurus
- Too many teeth?
- Sturdy skulls
- Number one dino
- Tail titan
- Mum's the word
- Crest champion
- Bonkers big
- More incredible dinosaur records

- Explosive eruption
- Wave power
- Dusty and dry
- So many species
- Speedy breeze
- Mighty mountain
- Cool as ice
- Burn, baby, burn
- Champion coral
- Dark depths
- Waterfall wonder
- Plant power
- More incredible Earth records

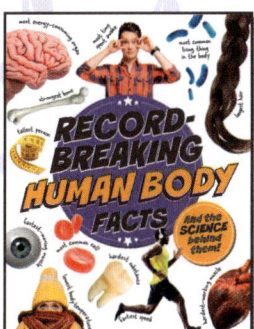

- Prize-winning pumping
- Feeling sleepy?
- Brain drain
- Almost freezing
- Mega-fast muscle
- So many cells
- Not so small
- Deep breath in ...
- Hard as a ... tooth?
- Rocket-powered run
- Baby bones
- Body invaders
- More incredible human body records

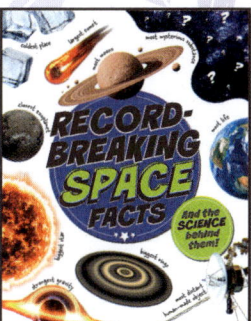

- A real superstar
- Short days
- Far, far away
- A powerful pull
- Roaming robots
- Mega rings
- Alive and kicking
- Space neighbour
- Strange substance
- Hot and cold
- So many moons
- Life lift-off
- More incredible space records

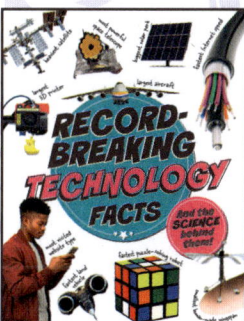

- Too big to fly?
- Champion clicks
- Deep, deep down
- Solid and sturdy
- Prize processors
- Let it shine
- (Nearly!) supersonic speed
- Seeing in space
- Fabulous fliers
- King of the printers
- Whizzy WiFi
- Super satellite
- More incredible technology records